Original title:
Rustles in the Rhododendrons

Copyright © 2025 Creative Arts Management OÜ
All rights reserved.

Author: Harris Montgomery
ISBN HARDBACK: 978-1-80567-385-9
ISBN PAPERBACK: 978-1-80567-684-3

Glistening Petals in the Morning Dew

Beneath the sun, the petals dance,
The bees do twirl, in a merry prance.
A squirrel sneezes, what a fright,
As butterflies play tag in sunlight.

The blooms all giggle, a sight to behold,
They chat of adventures, or so I've been told.
With colors so bright, they throw a fit,
As a grumpy snail slides, a little bit.

The canvas drips with morning's cheer,
While ladybugs cheer from the rear.
"Oh, what a day!" they all shout aloud,
As a wandering leaf flops, feeling proud.

The breeze giggles, with whispers of fun,
While water droplets have their own run.
Who knew a garden could bring such delight,
With chatter and chuckles that start with daylight!

Serenity Awaits in Floral Abodes

Among the blooms, a bee takes flight,
Chasing dreams in pure delight.
Giggling petals sway in jest,
Telling secrets at their best.

A snail slips by, all suave with flair,
Wearing shells with charming care.
The daisies wink, while roses blush,
In this haven, all is hush.

Secrets of the Blooming Sanctuary

In shady spots, the fairies play,
Trading jokes in bright array.
A curious bud eavesdrops near,
Writing tales for all to hear.

Laughter floats on breezy trails,
Where daffodils swap humorous tales.
The sunbeam's grin, a cheeky tease,
Spills joy through the dancing leaves.

A Whispered Promise in the Garden's Silence

Petunias gossip, soft and sweet,
While mischief stirs beneath their feet.
A quirky cat leaps, then trips,
Landing right amongst the slips.

With every bloom, a chuckle shared,
In every thorn, a trick prepared.
Oh, how they plot in leafy nooks,
Preparing jokes in secret books.

Harmonies Wrapped in Floral Elegance

The violets hum, a silly tune,
While butterflies dance 'neath the moon.
Chirping crickets join the band,
Creating laughs across the land.

With tulips sipping tea so grand,
And a sunbeam tickling the sand.
In the garden, a joyful spree,
Where nature's laughter sets us free.

The Poetry of Shadows and Light

In the garden, shadows creep,
A squirrel's secret, I must keep.
He wears a hat made of a leaf,
Confused, he thinks he's quite the chief.

The flowers chuckle, petals sway,
The sunlight dances, bright and gay.
A butterfly wears shades, it seems,
Diving low to catch sunbeams.

Mysteries Lurking in the Floral Depths

Beneath the blooms, a whisper calls,
A gnome is hiding, trying to stall.
With mismatched socks, he guards his prize,
A golden acorn, oh what a surprise!

Bees in fancy jackets buzz,
Announcing parties just because.
They trip on nectar, what a sight,
Stumbling home through the fading light.

A Dance of Colors on Gentle Paths

On winding trails, a rainbow skips,
While daisies gossip, sharing quips.
A peacock struts with flair and glow,
Flaunting colors just to show.

Ladybugs join in the fun,
Rolling 'round like they just won.
Their tiny laughter fills the air,
Wings a-tremble, without a care.

The Quietude of Nature's Embrace

Tall trees whisper, 'Hush, be still,'
While bunnies dig, they find a thrill.
A snail conducts the slow parade,
In clumsy moves, he's unafraid.

The breeze carries a joke from afar,
That makes the daisies giggle and spar.
In serene corners, laughter flows,
Nature's secret, nobody knows.

Blossoms Weaving Stories with the Wind

Petals giggle as they dance,
Telling tales of a heart's romance.
Butterflies join in the fray,
Twisting and twirling their bright ballet.

Bees buzz in their tiny fleet,
Searching for something sweet to eat.
A silly squirrel takes a leap,
While dreaming of treasures to keep.

The sun shines down, all aglow,
Winking at blooms in a row.
Laughter echoes through the trees,
As flowers nod with gentle ease.

In this garden, joy is found,
Where every chuckle spins around.
Nature's playground, pure delight,
With whispers shared from day to night.

The Enchantment of Flora and Fauna

Daisies sway with a jaunty flair,
While hummingbirds hover in midair.
A raccoon struts with a faux tux,
Thinking he's suave, but just a bit bucks.

Lilies laugh, their petals wide,
As frogs croak tunes with a sense of pride.
The dragonflies dart in quick retreat,
Playing tag with the grass, oh what a feat!

Chirpy crickets join the song,
While the flowers sing along.
Nature's cabaret, under the sun,
Where every creature joins the fun.

With blossoms twirling, oh so grand,
In a whimsical, wild band.
Together they frolic and play,
Turning evening into a bright ballet.

Breezes Caressing the Velvet Buds

Gentle whispers in the air,
Tickle leaves without a care.
Dandelions pop up with glee,
Playing hide and seek with the bee.

A chubby rabbit hops nearby,
His floppy ears can touch the sky.
He wiggles his nose, then takes a break,
Dreaming of carrot cake for goodness' sake!

Winds weave tales through budding blooms,
As laughter spills from hidden rooms.
The scent of mischief fills the air,
As petals cheer and giggle with flair.

Nature's jesters in bright attire,
Spreading joy, hearts never tire.
In this playful, breezy land,
Every moment is simply grand.

Petals Talking to the Playful Breeze

Whispers swirl with fragrant cheer,
As blossoms gossip, loud and clear.
The breeze, a friend, swings by to chat,
About the silly antics of that fat cat.

Lilacs chuckle, their scent divine,
While daisies share tales, oh so fine.
A butterfly winks with a fluttering wing,
Join our laughter, let's dance and sing!

The winds carry secrets of the day,
As leaves join in the merry play.
Nature's laughter, a joyous sound,
In every corner of this ground.

With petals grinning, sunbeams glow,
A whimsical show, a vibrant flow.
Together they tickle the afternoon,
As flowers and breezes hum a tune.

Sighs of the Sylvan Grove

In the woodlands where squirrels prance,
Leaves chatter softly, a leafy dance.
Breezes giggle, they tickle the trees,
While pinecones drop, oh, do they tease!

Foxes whisper their dinner plans,
As rabbits stare, in curious cans.
The mossy stones have secrets to tell,
In this vibrant forest, all is well.

Mysteries Among the Blossoms

Petals flutter like tiny socks,
While bees engage in their buzzing talks.
Daisies gossip about the sun,
'He's so bright, it's too much fun!'

Ladybugs wear their polka dots,
As ants parade in perfect knots.
With every bloom, a joke is sprouted,
The garden's tales are wise and crowded.

Serenade of the Leafy Shadows

In dappled light, the shadows play,
Frogs croak tunes, in their own way.
The branches sway like dancers so bold,
While stories weave from whispers old.

A turtle strains to join the dance,
With every step, it takes a chance.
Chirping crickets tune the night,
Under a moon so round and bright.

Softly Spoken in the Green

Beneath the canopy, creatures scheme,
Squirrels plotting their acorn dream.
Fungi giggle in their little caps,
Oh what fun, these nature laps!

The wind tells jokes with a gentle sigh,
While shadows flutter, oh me, oh my!
Every rustle holds a giggling clue,
In the heart of green, fun is true.

Hush of the Verdant Vale

In a leafy nook, a squirrel spun,
Chasing shadows, oh what fun!
With acorns flying, heard a clatter,
While birds chuckled at the matter.

A gnome with a hat that wobbled too,
Tripped over roots in morning dew.
The daisies laughed, their petals bright,
As he stumbled off in sheer delight.

A butterfly wearing shades so cool,
Danced with a beetle, quite the fool.
They twirled and spun without a care,
While frogs croaked tales of love to share.

The sunbeams played, a golden game,
Tickling leaves, igniting flame.
In this vale, where nonsense thrives,
Nature's comedy truly arrives.

Murmurs Through the Thicket

In the thicket where whispers tease,
A hedgehog snorted, lost in ease.
The rabbits giggled, tails a-fluff,
While the fox just rolled, not quite tough.

Amidst the bushes, a secret rave,
A raccoon led, oh how they gave!
With clapping paws and stomping feet,
They danced to rhythms, oh so sweet.

The bushes shook with laughter loud,
As chatter filled the merry crowd.
Even the trees did sway and grin,
How wonderful mischief can begin!

With snickers creeping under the boughs,
And laughter echoing through the browse,
Nature's jesters perform their art,
In this thicket, a vibrant heart.

Dance of the Forest Flora

Amid the blooms, a flower's jest,
With petals swirling, felt so blessed,
A daffodil wore goggles high,
As bees zipped past, just flying by.

The roses blushed, a giggling crew,
While daisies planned a bright-hued coup.
In every corner, mischief lurked,
In this garden, fun's berserk!

In shadows deep, a tulip twirled,
The dainty greens began to whirled,
With a wind that tickled every sprout,
Twirling, spinning, what's this about?

Petals flung in playful cheer,
As critters nudged and drew quite near.
The flora waltzed, and earth sighed too,
This dance was for all, both me and you.

Enigmatic Flora's Song

In verdant glades where secrets hum,
There blooms a plant that's quite the drum.
With leafy arms that stretch and bow,
It sings with laughter, take a vow.

A chant about roots and wiggly worms,
While butterflies showcase their twirly turns.
Even the moss joins in the tune,
As leaves do sway beneath the moon.

From fragrant petals, giggles leak,
Spreading joy that's far from meek.
A dandelion, with seeds aflight,
Wishes on breezes throughout the night.

In this enchanted, vibrant throng,
Every whisper is a happy song.
For in this place of joyous cheer,
Flora's humor brings us near.

Moonlit Conversations Among the Leaves

In the quiet night, the branches sway,
Squirrels gossip in a leafy ballet.
The moon listens in, a gracious host,
As whispers of mischief delight the most.

A raccoon retells tales, quite a feat,
Of stealing snacks and dodging defeat.
While owls hoot laughter, a soft round of cheer,
In the world of the whisperers, all is clear.

Sighs of the Garden's Heart

Petunias chuckle, shaking their heads,
As tulips complain of overcooked breads.
Daisies giggle at the drama of blooms,
While violets dance in their bright paper costumes.

A bee buzzes in, with tales of his flight,
Of flower romances under the moonlight.
The roses roll eyes, sharing knowing looks,
As the garden unfolds its humorous books.

The Serenade of Blossoms and Whispers

A melody hums through the sprouting greens,
As daisies debate their best dancing scenes.
The lilacs join in, with a tune of their own,
While dandelions burst out, seeds lightly blown.

With petals ablaze, they sway to the beat,
Scaring away ants in their comical feet.
Giggling together, the blooms find their joy,
In a garden where laughter sprout with each ploy.

Beneath the Canopy of Color

Under vivid hues, the insects convene,
Sharing the tales of what they've seen.
A beetle rolls laughter, a silly old chap,
While ladybugs snicker in sunny warm lap.

The trees quiver softly, exchanging their quirks,
As flowers create rhymes, with laughter that lurks.
In the tapestry bright, their merriment swells,
Where humor and nature weave all their spells.

Dreams Adrift in Flowered Halls

In a garden where whispers tease,
The blooms gossip in a breeze.
A daffodil sneezes with flair,
While a rose tries hard not to share.

Butterflies wear party hats,
As bees dance like fancy bats.
Petunias giggle, petals aglow,
While daisies play peek-a-boo in a row.

A tulip trips over its shoe,
Losing its focus, a comical view.
With roots in a tangle, oh dear,
They laugh about it, no sign of fear.

Each flower hums a silly tune,
Beneath the watchful eye of the moon.
In this joyful, leafy retreat,
Every blossom knows how to be sweet.

Hidden Harmonies of the Bush

In thickets where laughter is born,
A squirrel debates with the thorn.
"Who's pricklier?" it tosses a nut,
While the brambles giggle, cheeky and shut.

Mischief brews in the leafy thrum,
As critters plan their next silly drum.
Why did the rabbit cross the way?
To show off his dance or earn a bouquet?

The hedgehog rolls, a spiky ball,
Inviting all to a joyful sprawl.
With chatter echoing sharp and bright,
The whole bush joins in, a raucous delight.

Here in the greens, secrets unfold,
As every twig has a tale retold.
Laughter mingles with rustling leaves,
In harmony where the bush believes.

Lullabies of the Flourishing Wilderness

In the woods where mischief plays,
A raccoon juggles twigs most days.
While owl gives a hoot of cheer,
What a night when laughter draws near!

The mushrooms form a laughing band,
With tiny hats, all perfectly planned.
Singing sweetly beneath the stars,
The forest grooves with its silly guitars.

A fox with style, flamboyant strut,
Steals the scene, oh what a nut!
With each leaf, a chuckle escapes,
As humor bounces between the drapes.

Lullabies drip from the trees,
With ticklish breezes that aim to please.
The wilderness, in a joyful trance,
Dances around in a carefree prance.

Tread Lightly on the Ferns

Amidst the ferns, a secret crew,
Composed of critters, comes into view.
A snail races, slow and sly,
While a frog leaps, reaching for the sky.

Nature's jesters wear leafy crowns,
Spreading giggles through happy towns.
The moss hums softly, keeping pace,
As a lizard joins the merry chase.

A rabbit trips, but takes a bow,
Remarking, "Oh dear, now wow!"
Each tumble grows laughter loud,
Underneath a fluffy cloud.

So tread lightly, adventure awaits,
Every step leads to funny debates.
With each rustle, a chuckle near,
Nature's comedy is sincere.

Whispers of the Wild Blooms

Bumblebees are buzzing loud,
With secret plots to cheer the crowd.
Petals wiggle in the breeze,
Each one laughs, they aim to please.

Butterflies don silly stunts,
Dancing high, they're playful brunts.
A sneaky snail makes his way,
Pretending he's in a ballet.

Mice in hats throw a grand spree,
When the sun sets, they shout with glee.
Every blossom has its tricks,
In this garden, laughter clicks.

So gather round, and heed the call,
The wild blooms play, they have a ball.
Join the mirth, don't miss the fun,
In a world where joy has spun.

Secrets Beneath the Canopy

Under leaves where mischief brews,
Giggling critters share their views.
Squirrels boasting of their finds,
While chatting about clever minds.

The mushrooms wear their polka dots,
Raccoons plotting sneaky spots.
Chirping birds play hide and seek,
A game they think is quite unique.

Crickets hum a silly tune,
While dancing 'neath the silver moon.
Each shadow casts a playful glance,
Encouraging a cheeky dance.

So wander softly, take a peek,
These woodland pals are far from meek.
Their giggles linger in the air,
In the canopy, fun's everywhere.

Echoes Among the Petals

In the thicket, whispers roam,
Each flower bids a happy welcome home.
Daisies roll their eyes with glee,
Judging bees who took too long for tea.

A dragonfly with feathered flair,
Flits around without a care.
He charms the blooms with jokes so grand,
While daisies snicker, just as planned.

Flowerpots are not what they seem,
They've got tales that make you beam.
Rubber plants do backflips bold,
When the sun sets, their stories unfold.

So listen close, let laughter thrive,
Among the petals, all alive.
A giggle here, a chuckle there,
In echoes, joy is everywhere.

Shadows in Blooming Glades

In a glade where shadows play,
Sunny blooms have much to say.
Petal pirates on the prowl,
Stealing sunshine with a howl.

Lilies gossip, what a sight!
Talking trash in pure delight.
A playful breeze joins in their cheer,
Tickling leaves from far and near.

Whimsical weeds throw a parade,
With dainty cups, their plans are made.
While butterflies recite their tricks,
Causing blooms to crack up in clicks.

So meander through this joyful maze,
The shadows dance, a vibrant haze.
In blooming glades where laughter sways,
Every whisper brings a sunny phase.

Hushed Voices of the Arboretum

In the garden, whispers play,
Bumblebees dance, hip-hip-hooray!
Squirrels gossip, tails in a twirl,
While flowers giggle, give a whirl.

Sunlight winks, it paints the scene,
Ladybugs plotting, oh so keen!
The trees sway like they're in a trance,
As petals ponder a leafy dance.

A snail slips by, oh what a fuss,
In this realm, it's quite a plus!
With all this chatter, who needs a tune?
The forest hums an endless croon.

So let's laugh with the branches high,
Join in the fun and don't be shy!
For in this place where voices blend,
Nature's humor knows no end.

Nature's Secret Symphony

Crickets strum a nightly band,
With frogs on keys, a sight so grand!
Trees tap dance, roots all aglow,
While owls hoot in a feathery show.

The wind hums low, a cheeky tune,
As flowers sway, in playful swoon.
A chipmunk joins with a sweet refrain,
Chasing shadows, running down the lane.

A raccoon claps, with paws so fine,
To this wild beat, he's feeling divine!
With laughter echoing through the trees,
Nature's music floats with ease.

So come, partake in this lively spree,
Where even the branches giggle with glee,
For in this world of vibrant delight,
The notes of nature take flight each night.

Poems in the Shade of Petals

Beneath the blooms, a riddle spins,
With petals whispering of wins and sins.
A butterfly flutters, a drama queen,
While daisies chuckle, the liveliest scene.

The bugs convene for a comedy show,
With puns aplenty, whoosh, here they go!
Each blossom knows the punchline well,
As laughter echoes through nature's spell.

A beetle jives with that fanciful grace,
Roses roll their eyes in this bustling place.
And in the shade where the humor grows,
The plants trade tales that nobody knows.

So come sit down, join this vast parade,
Where every leaf has a joke well laid,
In nature's chamber, fun will ensue,
Beneath the petals, laughs like dew.

Quietude Among the Rays

In morning light, the giggles start,
With sunbeams dancing, oh what art!
The daisies wave, in a silly cheer,
As bumblebees buzz, lending an ear.

A rabbit pops in, with mischief in mind,
While lilacs joke, ever so kind.
The breeze carries tales of every sort,
As trees play games, as if in court.

With laughter sprinkled on petals bright,
Every moment feels perfectly light.
A garden of humor, spread wide and far,
Nature's own laughter is quite the star.

So linger a while, bask in the fun,
With joy in the shade, the day's just begun!
For in this quiet, where beams brightly lay,
The heart of the garden will whimsically sway.

Threads of Life in the Floral Web

In the garden where giggles bloom,
A squirrel starts dancing, eclipsing the gloom.
With tussles and tumbles, it leaps with grace,
Chasing clouds or just its own furry face.

Petals parade with whispering flair,
Bees break-dance above without a care.
The flowers join in with a swaying jig,
As ants conga line, oh, what a gig!

Ladybugs laugh in spots of red,
While caterpillars nibble on leafy bread.
The wind teases blossoms to twirl and spin,
Creating a ruckus, where all life begins.

Nature throws parties, come join the fun,
Where even the shadows have a chance to run.
So tiptoe, skip, or jump, just don't stroll,
You'll find laughter springs from the earth's very soul.

Beacons of Color in Nature's Palette

A rainbow sprinkles joy, oh so bright,
As sunflowers wave like flags in delight.
Marigolds giggle in gold, taking stance,
While violets whisper, 'Come join the dance!'

Tulips decked in hats of fine cloth,
Invite the butterflies, come take a swath.
Daffodils jump with a cheerful cheer,
Saying, 'Life's a party, fill it with cheer!'

A painter's palette spreads wide with glee,
With every brushstroke, nature's decree.
Swaying petals wink like mischievous sprites,
A canvas of laughter, pure festivity bites.

So grab a paintbrush, take to the hills,
Join nature's canvas, let joy be your thrills.
For every hue shared, a chuckle is spun,
In this garden where every day's fun!

Tales Told by the Bird's Sweet Song

In the treetops, a tune starts to play,
Birds chirp, gossip, in a delightful spray.
Each notes a tale, woven light as a feather,
Of seeds, of sprinkles, and light spring weather.

A finch sings of crumbs from yesterday's feast,
While sparrows exchange tales, to say the least.
"Oh, did you see? The worm wiggled quick!"
Laughter erupts as they share every trick.

The lullaby shifts, a hoot from afar,
A wise old owl claims, "I'm the true star!"
While robins, in chorus, sing songs of cheer,
Weaving their stories for all who can hear.

Tap your heels to a symphony divine,
Nature's orchestra plays, it's simply sublime!
The tales float high on a wing and a breeze,
Bringing smiles and giggles with effortless ease.

The Heartbeat of Wilderness Unveiled

The woods are alive with a comedic beat,
As trees tell jokes with their roots in the heat.
A bear in a bowtie takes the stage,
His stand-up act a true woodland rage!

Squirrels chime in with their nutty puns,
While raccoons juggle and keep score with runs.
'Why did the tree join a comedy club?'
'It wanted to leave all its troubles in a shrub!'

The brook laughs softly, a giggling stream,
As frogs croak punchlines, bringing a beam.
With flowers as audience, their petals aflutter,
It's a wild show where smiles never utter.

Come laugh with the forest, where fun never ends,
Where nature's heart dances and joy transcends.
So give a loud cheer for the mirth all around,
In this cheerful wild world, happiness found!

Stories Carried on the Wind's Breath

Whispers tickle leaves up high,
While squirrels plot a nutty heist.
The breeze giggles, clouds roll by,
As nature plays, oh such a feast!

A flower sings in laughing tones,
While bees buzz, joining in the fun.
They dance among the leafy thrones,
And tease the sun till day is done.

A dandelion, a tiny puff,
Gets carried by the wind so free.
It dreams of journeys, oh so tough,
Yet lands on a kid's nose with glee!

So gather round, and listen close,
For tales that nature loves to share.
With giggles, grins, and grandiose,
The world outside is filled with flair.

A Symphony in the Petal's Heart

In the garden, petals sway,
Like a band on a sunny stage.
Bumblebees hit a jazzy play,
As daisies bloom and engage.

A rose whistles a silly tune,
While lilacs join with fragrant notes.
The tulips sway beneath the moon,
Creating magic as life floats.

Each flower knows a secret beat,
A symphony of color bright.
The dancing leaves feel oh so sweet,
In petals' heart, pure delight.

With giggles sprouting everywhere,
The world turns wild with vibrant cheer.
Each bloom a laugh, each wind a dare,
A joyful song for all to hear.

Nature's Soft Secrets Unveiled

Under petals, secrets hide,
Whispering tales without a sound.
Ants march bravely side by side,
In search of treasures underground.

A butterfly, all dressed in style,
Winks at bees with a silly grin.
The sun peeks out, goes for a while,
Playing hide and seek with the wind.

A gentle breeze, a hidden jest,
As flowers giggle, one by one.
They share a chuckle, feeling blessed,
For in this game, we're all just fun!

So when you stroll through greens so bright,
Listen close and you may find.
The secrets of the day and night,
In nature's laughter, so aligned.

The Language of Blossoms in the Air

Blossoms chatter, a playful bunch,
In colors bright, their voices cheer.
Petals gossip over lunch,
While butterflies lend an eager ear.

The wind translates with a bold flair,
As blooms confess their dreams and schemes.
They laugh and dance without a care,
In the sunlight's warm, golden beams.

A daffodil leans in to share,
A story of a bumblebee's flight.
Each petal knows how to declare,
Life's little joys wrapped up in light.

So join the blooms and take your cue,
From whispers that the garden sings.
Life's a language weaves anew,
In every leaf, untamed with wings.

Murmurs of the Mountain Flowers

Beneath the boughs, they whisper low,
A tale of bees, and how they show.
Petals giggle in the sun,
A ticklish game of flower fun.

Frogs croak laughs as they pass by,
Making clouds of joy in sky.
A vibrant dance, a fragrant jest,
Nature's revelry at its best.

Leaves share secrets, oh so bold,
Of shy squirrels and their nuts of gold.
In this patch of blooming cheer,
Even grumpy rocks can hear.

So lift your cup, let laughter spill,
With every breeze, let joy fulfill.
In every bud, a chuckle's spun,
The mountains' mirth has just begun.

Hidden Voices in Petal Breezes

In the soft sway, they chime and hum,
Petals gossip, oh what fun!
Whiskered bees with silly prance,
Join the blooms in their wild dance.

A butterfly, with stylish flair,
Fluffs its wings in frilly air.
"It's my turn now," it seems to shout,
Buzzing bugs just knock about.

One flower slips, a stem-locked trip,
While others giggle, then they flip.
Laughter echoes off the trees,
Even the stones crack smiles with ease.

So join the jest, don't shy away,
Let the petals rule the day.
Breezes carry tales of cheer,
Nature's laugh floats ever near.

Hush of Spring's Midnight Melody

In the stillness, whispers play,
Crickets strum the night away.
Moonlit blooms sway soft and light,
Singing dreams till morning bright.

A wandering wisp steals the moment,
From sleepy buds to sweet torment.
Fireflies flicker, dance and tease,
Springtime's jest in the gentle breeze.

Secret songs of owls take flight,
While shadows giggle in the night.
Buds blink open, laughing loud,
Joining the merry midnight crowd.

So hush your heart, let silence gleam,
As the world plays in a dream.
For in the quiet, a spark ignites,
A symphony of whimsical nights.

Shadows Dancing with the Petal Light

Underneath the giant trees,
Shadows wiggle, dance with ease.
Petal parties, oh so bright,
Turn the day into a night!

A spider's web spins tales anew,
As tiny ants join the hullabaloo.
"Oh, flower friend, don't be shy,
Join our dance; let laughter fly!"

Bouncing beetles, oh what cheer!
Twirling 'round as dusk draws near.
The joy in blooms, a hearty sight,
Playing tricks in fading light.

So bounce along, take up your chance,
With every twirl, join nature's dance.
In the garden, fun's in bloom,
A riot of giggles fills the room.

Tales Beneath the Green Veil

In a tangle of leaves, squirrels prance,
Rabbits hop about, in their fanciful dance.
They plot little mischief behind the bark,
Whispers of laughter echo in the park.

Underneath branches both leafy and wide,
A band of bugs formed a funny side.
In tiny tuxedos, they wiggled with glee,
Oh, the tales they spun, just wait and see.

Amidst all the blooms, a snail took a race,
And stumbled on petals in a dizzy embrace.
A ladybug laughed 'til her spots were in rows,
As pollen went flying from a bee's clumsy pose.

They gather at dusk with their giggles and cheer,
As shadows grow long, and the night draws near.
Yet in the stillness, their secret is told,
In the whisper of leaves, lies the laughter of old.

The Color of Quietude

Under the shade, a frog croaks a tune,
While a bee interrupts with a bold little swoon.
The air is alive with a vibrant report,
As a bright butterfly starts a little court.

Twisting and turning, the garden's in glee,
Dancing with joys as easy as can be.
The daisies all giggle, the tulips look shocked,
At a tall sunflower in a wig made of broccoli and locked.

A hedgehog stumbles over bags of sweet peas,
Wearing a crown made of fallen tree leaves.
They gathered 'round gossip with roots all aglow,
In a world of bright colors, who knew? Just so!

Lost in a daydream, the petals then sway,
Telling their stories in their own funny way.
Their whispers grow louder, full of bragging rights,
As night adds a hush, and the laughter ignites.

Beneath the Veil of Petals

A plucky old turtle races the breeze,
While a mouse on a skateboard lands near the trees.
With petals for pillows, they lounge with delight,
Chasing dreams and bugs, in the soft moonlight.

In wonder they ponder the game of tag,
With ants in two pairs, looking rather ragged.
Not too far off, a giggling chickadee,
Keeps score in chirps, isn't it funny? Hee-hee!

The garden's a circus of wild, crazy fun,
As the insects and critters blend with the sun.
They try out new tricks, with a wink and a leap,
In a symphony of chaos, the nighttime creeps.

So cheers rise like blooms at the height of their chance,
A toast from the flowers, as they wiggle and dance.
For beneath the bright colors, their stories unfold,
In laughter and joy, there's magic to behold.

Fluttering Silhouettes in Bloom

Fluttering figures flit here and there,
With jests wrapped in petals, and fun in the air.
A chubby old bug dons a top hat so grand,
While the daisies stand proud, with a giggle, they stand.

A chatter of critters in a busy bee's hive,
Plotting a party to keep spirits alive.
The ferns sway and rustle, trying to hear,
As the mischief unfolds, drawing all near.

A thief in the night, a raccoon on the roam,
Steals a bright lantern from a garden full-blown.
The fireflies flash warnings of danger and doom,
Yet chuckles erupt like a bright blossoming bloom.

So gather around for the fun and surprise,
Beneath the green mantle where laughter will rise.
In this garden of quirks, let your spirit take flight,
For joy is the bloom that shines brightest at night.

Lullabies from the Leafy Thicket

In the thicket where leaves play,
A squirrel sings at the break of day.
His voice is squeaky, like a toy,
Making mischief with utter joy.

The branches sway in a bumbling dance,
As worms wiggle in a goofy trance.
A ladybug twirls in a bright red dress,
While a frog croaks out, 'I'm a bit of a mess!'

The shadows giggle, the flowers giggle louder,
A bumblebee buzzes, trying to powder.
With every bloom, a silly grin,
In this thicket, no frown can win.

So if you're lost and need a chuckle,
Just follow the sounds of nature's shuffle.
In leafy corners, laughter brews,
As critters create their own morning news.

Songs of the Silken Blooms

The petals sway like they're in a band,
Dancing to tunes from a clumsy hand.
A bee takes the mic, but it's pure buzz,
Mistaking the crowd for a big ol' fuzz.

A butterfly flutters, lost in a trance,
Catching the rhythm, eager to prance.
But oops! It lands right on a nose,
Who knew a flower could tickle, goodness knows!

The daisies clap in their own way,
While tulips blush at the on-display.
Geraniums giggle at the jiving lip,
As daisies tumble, taking a slip.

In this garden, joy's not shy,
Every bloom is a singer, oh my!
With songs that echo and bubble with glee,
Nature's concert, a hilarity spree.

The Kiss of Dawn on Velvet Pines

As dawn tiptoes on velvet green,
The pines yawn wide, their faces serene.
But one tree sneezes, big and loud,
Sending squirrels scampering, scared and proud.

The sun peeks in, a golden eye,
Winking at clouds passing by.
A raccoon smirks, munching on a snack,
While a chipmunk chirps, 'We've got no lack!'

Dewdrops glisten like tiny pearls,
As giggles echo from the spinning swirls.
Nature's cheeky side comes alive,
With every rustle, the forest thrives.

So if you wander where pines stand tall,
Listen closely to their lullaby call.
In morning rays, a silly plot,
A symphony of fun in every spot.

Gentle Breezes Over Floral Dreams

Breezes tickle the petals' cheek,
As flowers gossip, hear them speak.
'Is that a moth or just a blur?'
The roses giggle, 'It's quite a stir!'

A dandelion's fluff takes flight,
Wandering off in pure delight.
A heavy bee thinks it's a ride,
Crashing down when he takes a glide.

The lilies laugh, the violets wink,
Creating mischief, what do you think?
With pollen hats and dazzling flair,
These flower folk have dreams to share.

So sway with laughter, drift and stream,
In gentle breezes of floral dream.
When nature's giggles fill the air,
You'll find joy is everywhere!

The Unseen Conversations of Greenery.

In the shade where leaves conspire,
Caterpillars plot to wear attire.
They chat of colors, bold and bright,
While squirrels snicker, teasing their plight.

The trees gossip in the gentle breeze,
Sharing tales of sun and tease.
One says, 'Did you see the bee?'
Another replies, 'Oh, what a sight to see!'

Flowers giggle, twirling in glee,
Talking 'bout how lovely they'd be.
But roses pout, their thorns in a huff,
'Why can't they see? I'm pretty enough!'

A breeze walks by, a playful friend,
Spreading rumors that never end.
'Did you hear the bird? Oh, what a fluke!'
Laughter echoes through each leafy nook.

Whispers Beneath the Blooming Canopy

Beneath the greens, secrets sprout,
Daisy whispers, without a doubt.
'This shade's my throne, can't you see?'
While dewdrops giggle, wild and free.

The bumblebee packs lunch for the day,
But forgets where his meal is, oh, what a fray!
The flowers snicker, 'He's lost it again!'
As he flies round and round like a confused hen.

Leaves rustle softly, mimicking sighs,
As butterflies tease, 'Look, I can fly!'
But one thudded down, quite a sight,
And the others chortled, 'Well, that's not right!'

In the midst of blooms, laughter swells,
Echoes of joy, where nature dwells.
A silly saga, sung without pause,
Life in the grove, is full of guffaws!

Secrets Tucked Among the Blossoms

Among the petals, secrets do hide,
A chatty sparrow thinks he's a guide.
'Follow me, my little crew!'
While the shy snails say, 'No, thank you!'

The violets gossip about the new daffodil,
'Her dance isn't graceful, but it's full of thrill!'
But giggles are quiet when she twirls around,
As a rogue gust of wind knocks her down to the ground.

Hiding behind petals, a ladybug takes a peek,
She's heard all the jokes and feels quite unique.
'Who needs a crown, when you're so chic?'
The blooms are applauding, 'Come shine, don't be meek!'

In corners of green, laughter's the tune,
The jokes bloom brightly beneath the bright moon.
Amongst the shadows, they chuckle with flair,
The secrets they share float high in the air.

Echoes of the Enchanted Grove

In the grove where summer's found,
Laughter bounces all around.
A frog croaks jokes; a tree topsy-turvy,
It seems that nature feels quite wavy.

Buds bob their heads, quite in sync,
As the wind tickles leaf edges, they wink.
'What's green and funny?' whispers a vine,
A round of giggles, 'Oh, where's the punchline?'

The sun peeps through, casting joyful rays,
Illuminating the antics of playful ballets.
A wise old owl hoots from high above,
'You all are sillier than a dove!'

With echoes of chuckles marking the trees,
Each twist and turn brings nature's tease.
In this grove, where fun finds its way,
Every leaf dances, come night or day!

Hues of Joy in the Woodland Nook

In the woods where laughter plays,
A squirrel dances, lost in a craze.
He twirled and spun, quite the sight,
Chasing shadows in the sweet daylight.

The flowers giggle, quite absurd,
As the bees buzz off, their wings unheard.
A rabbit trips on its floppy ears,
But laughs it off, no room for fears.

The trees murmur secrets, wise and old,
While a deer struts, its heart so bold.
A chorus of chirps in a playful feast,
Nature's humor never ceased.

With colors bright amidst the glee,
A wild parade, just wait and see.
From reds to yellows, all in the fun,
Dancing together, hearts on the run.

Nature's Diary Amidst Blooming Hues

In the meadow where the daisies giggle,
A butterfly winks, it even does a jiggle.
Grasshoppers hop, their tunes so slick,
While a snail schemes, thinking it's quick.

The clouds play peek-a-boo with the sun,
As toads begin their croak-a-thon run.
A flower sneezes, oh, what a mess,
Leaves scatter about in floral distress.

The brook chuckles as it flows by,
Whispering tales to clouds in the sky.
A mischievous wind takes a playful glee,
Twirling the leaves like it's their spree.

Oh, nature's diary, what laughs you hold,
With stories of whimsy, bright and bold.
Each page a chuckle, a twirl, a dance,
Inviting us all to join the chance.

Clusters of Color in a Dreaming Wood

In the wood where colors collide,
A snail hosts a party, come join the ride!
With every step, the mushrooms grin,
As the critters gather, let the fun begin!

The flowers wear hats, each one in style,
A dandelion prince with a cheeky smile.
The winds whisper jokes to the tall pine trees,
While ladybugs laugh, just doing as they please.

An owl in glasses reads to a crow,
Who caws back loudly, stealing the show.
The sun dips low, painting the night,
Squirrels in capes take off in flight!

Clusters of laughter fill the night air,
With fairies giggling at their own affair.
Nature's delight, a whimsical space,
Where joy is found in every place.

Untold Tales of the Garden's Gaze

In the garden where secrets bloom,
A hedgehog juggles with a flower's plume.
Roses blush at the sight so rare,
While tomatoes giggle without a care.

A bumblebee tickles the petal's face,
And a worm gets lost in an earthworm race.
The ivy whispers stories to the wall,
As a curious ant prepares for the ball.

Each bud holds tales of laugh and cheer,
As birds play hopscotch, never a fear.
The moon peeks down with a knowing grin,
Watching the chaos, where do we begin?

Untold tales in the soft moonlight,
In this garden of wonder, everything's bright.
The laughter lingers, sweet as a song,
In the heart of nature, where we belong.

Shadows Underneath the Flowered Arch

Beneath the blooms, a squirrel leaps,
Chasing shadows, making peeps.
A wily cat, with stealthy paws,
Laughs at the antics, with tiny claws.

The flowers giggle, swaying so bright,
At dancing bees' clumsy flight.
A jaybird caws, it's quite the sight,
As petals blush in morning light.

A rabbit hops, it trips on leaves,
While a snail writes stories, if one believes.
Butterflies argue, who flies the best?
Amidst this chaos, joy's a fest!

So find a spot, take a seat,
In the blossom's laughter, life's sweet treat.
With nature's jokes, all wrapped in green,
In this silly world, we're forever keen.

A Tapestry of Joy in Greenery

In a world where mushrooms wear hats,
And playful gnomes chase after rats.
The daisies wink with mischievous glee,
While ladybugs sip on herbal tea.

A butterfly golf, oh what a swing!
The wild asters cheer, as they cling.
The sunflowers smile, so wide and tall,
As grasshoppers break into a funny sprawl.

A romance blooms 'tween a bee and a rose,
They bicker sweetly, who chews the prose.
While in the back, a hedgehog snorts,
Over sharing tales of wild, quaint resorts.

This tapestry of laughter and bright hues,
Weaves together the quirks of nature's muse.
Join the revelry, let worries go,
In this splendid garden, let giggles flow.

Memory's Reflection in Petal Pools

In puddles of petals, a frog hops high,
With a crown of daisies, it feels like a guy.
The sunbeams dance on the gleeful scene,
As it croaks a tune, so silly and keen.

Reflections ripple with laughter's delight,
As a snail races past, oh what a sight!
He brags of his speed, but everyone knows,
He's slower than pollen that tickles the nose.

A ladybug's balance, on a silky thread,
Dances through air, where wild winds spread.
A mockingbird chimes with a comical twist,
In a concert of chaos, can't be missed!

Now gather 'round, for tales to tell,
Of frogs, snails, and pollen's spell.
In memory's warmth, we share a chuckle,
In the gardens of joy, where laughter's a shuffle.

Voices of the Wildflowers' Dreams

The wildflowers chatter, their secrets exchanged,
About the bear who mistakenly changed.
A tumbleweed rolls, tickled by breeze,
While chatting daisies boast about cheese.

A vixen prances, with flair and wit,
While mushrooms quake, and giggle a bit.
The sunflowers gossip in colors so bright,
Over bloom ballads that spark sheer delight.

Petunias whisper of dreams gone absurd,
Of fancy unicorns and a talking bird.
The violets chuckle, their laughter so light,
In a symphony of giggles, pure-hearted and bright.

So come to the meadow, where joy takes flight,
Where flowers converse 'neath the moonlight.
In their voices, echoes of dreams unconfined,
A tapestry woven, so silly, so kind.

Traces of Summer's Sweet Secrets

In the garden, bees do hum,
With whispers soft as cotton candy,
A squirrel in a trunk, a little clumsy,
Dropping acorns, oh so handy.

The flowers giggle, petals shake,
A poke from a daisy, a sweet mistake,
"Who put the garden hose there?" they tease,
"Watch your step, or you'll be on your knees!"

A gnome in shades, he does a jig,
While butterflies float like a funny fig,
The sun winks down, "What a sight!"
In this quirky garden, all feels right.

So let's dance with the blooms so bright,
Chasing shadows in joyful light,
For in this patch of joy we hide,
Summer's secrets, our playful guide.

Whispers of Love in the Flora

Two tulips gossip by the gate,
"One's too shy, the other's late!"
"Do you think the roses know?
About the way the daisies glow?"

A bumblebee with quite the buzz,
Claims he's won a flower's fuzz,
With petals soft and pollen sweet,
He struts around on tiny feet.

The violets wink, the lilies cheer,
"Take your time, the coast is clear!"
In this patch, love's a game,
Where blooms and bugs all feel the same.

So let them chat, let laughter flow,
In the garden where romances grow,
For even flowers need a chance,
To join in on this silly dance.

Echoes of Laughter in the Green Realm

In a nook where sunlight beams,
The flowers plot their silly schemes,
"Let's tickle the toes of wading birds,
And share our jokes with everyone's words!"

A wind that's playful spins around,
Chasing leaves that laugh, unbound,
"Did you hear the one about the tree?"
"Not a single leaf knew, that's the glee!"

Frogs croak jokes from the lily pads,
While squirrels giggle, oh so glad,
"Did you see that cat, what a fright!
Chasing a shadow in midday light!"

In this green realm, laughter's free,
With echoes bouncing, wild as can be,
So join the fun beneath the sky,
Where joy will flutter, never shy.

The Dance of Sunlight on Petals

The sun peeks in, a playful tease,
Making petals shimmy in the breeze,
"Hey there, daisies, show some flair,
Let's spin and twirl without a care!"

Lilies's sway with quite the grace,
While sunflowers turn, a beaming face,
"We're the stars of this garden show,
Watch our dance, come join the flow!"

Butterflies flutter, clumsily they prance,
In the midst of this floral dance,
"Who knew petals could get so wild?"
With laughter ringing, oh so mild.

Let the sunlight paint our day,
With colors bright in a merry way,
For in this garden, joy's embraced,
A waltz of beauty, never replaced.

The Scent of Serenity in Nature's Embrace

Birch trees dance with silly glee,
While squirrels plan their comedy spree.
Bumblebees buzz in a high-pitched tune,
Hoping to charm a flowered monsoon.

Frogs croak jokes on lily pads bright,
Telling tales well into the night.
With each rustle, they share a quip,
As frogs and flowers take a sip.

The daisies giggle in morning light,
Tickled by breezes, oh what a sight!
Butterflies flutter as if to say,
"Join the party, come out and play!"

With every brush of green with yellow,
Nature's laugh is a joyful fellow.
Bring your smiles and leave your woes,
In this haven, merriment flows!

A Chorus of Life Amidst Petals

A ladybug struts in polka-dot pride,
While ants march by, organized wide.
Crickets chirp their own little song,
In a world where the silly belong.

Petals sway with a hip-hop beat,
Flowers shuffling their little feet.
Sunlight spills like lemonade sweet,
While bees bust moves, oh so neat!

The grass giggles, tickled by toes,
As the wind jokes, and everyone knows.
Nature's stage is where we're cast,
In this humorous charm, we're all amassed.

Chatting flowers trade puns galore,
With every gust, there's always more.
In this garden, laughter reigns true,
Life's punchlines are dressed in dew!

Voices of the Heart Among Earth's Tapestry

In the meadow, whispers of delight,
Grass blades laughing, oh what a sight!
The thrumming leaves tell stories anew,
Of squirrels and sparrows, and mischief too.

The petals gossip in colors so bright,
Trading secrets with the warm sunlight.
Mockingbirds mimic a laugh or two,
As the trees shake their branches anew.

Worms on a mission, wiggle and squirm,
Debating their paths in slinky form.
Every burrow holds a tale profound,
In this zany world, joy can be found.

With the rustle of grass, the tales unfold,
In this tapestry of life, brave and bold.
Nature's orchestra plays in sync,
In every breath, there's laughter to drink!

Garden Dreams in the Soft Twilight

As dusk tiptoes on shadows' parade,
Moonflowers giggle, their secrets conveyed.
Fireflies dance in a jig of light,
In this garden, the fun takes flight.

Crickets burst into a symphony grand,
With frogs providing an offbeat band.
The daffodils bow with petals aglow,
In twilight's embrace, they steal the show.

Each inch of the earth hums in delight,
Stars twinkle down, giggling at night.
With nightscapes painted in velvet hues,
This playful realm just oozes good views.

As dreams take shape in dusk's gentle grip,
Nature's punchlines make spirits zip.
Join the laughter, let worries take wing,
In this garden, hear the joy that we bring!

www.ingramcontent.com/pod-product-compliance
Lightning Source LLC
Chambersburg PA
CBHW070748220426
43209CB00083B/135